Pat Mayo

Sept. 15, 1978 -

MOCKINGBIRDS and ANGEL SONGS

MOCKINGBIRDS and ANGEL SONGS & OTHER PRAYERS

Jo Carr
and
Imogene Sorley

ABINGDON PRESS
Nashville New York

MOCKINGBIRDS AND ANGEL SONGS

Three selections are adapted from devotions by Jo Carr which have appeared in *United Methodists Today:* pp. 55-56 from the June, 1975 issue, copyright © 1975 by The United Methodist Publishing House; p. 57 from the April, 1974 issue, and pp. 58-59 from the August, 1974 issue, both copyright © 1974 by The United Methodist Publishing House.

Text quoted on p. 82 is from an ancient prayer. Poetry on p. 83 from "Flower in the Crannied Wall," by Alfred Tennyson. Two lines of poetry quoted on p. 90 are from James Weldon Johnson's poem "Listen, Lord–A Prayer" in *God's Trombones,* copyright 1927 by The Viking Press, Inc., copyright © renewed 1955 by Grace Nail Johnson, and are reprinted by permission of The Viking Press, Inc. Lines quoted on p. 94 are from Meister Eckhart.

Library of Congress Cataloging in Publication Data

CARR, JO.
Mockingbirds and angel songs and other prayers.

1. Prayers. I. Sorley, Imogene, joint author.
II. Title.
BV245.C324 242'.8 75-11847

ISBN 0-687-27099-5

MANUFACTURED BY THE PARTHENON PRESS AT NASHVILLE, TENNESSEE, UNITED STATES OF AMERICA

Dear Lord,

A mockingbird has sung for me all the pleasant afternoon, and I have sat here, hands busy shelling peas, heart free to enjoy his song. He has practiced a lilting variety of soaring, rippling bits of tunes, borrowed from other birds.

But he ended his concert, just now, unworthily . . . with a six-bar rendition of raucous squeals—readily recognized as our guinea pig's supper call. Squeals—that's all—an imperative monotone of gravelly squeals, practiced, I suppose, until he achieved such perfect imitation.

Technically an achievement—
but aesthetically unbecoming to a mockingbird.

Do you *wonder* at us, Lord, when we work diligently to copy unworthy models? When we *practice* the most raucous of the sounds we hear —we, who might just as well copy from angel song?

Likely so.

Father, forgive our sheer stupidity!

Amen.

Lord,
I've been thinking about that eyelash that got in my eye last night—nearly drove me frantic. It hurt outrageously, for such a little thing—and, for a time, rendered me blind.

It's not as though it had been a speck of "foreign matter." This was *my eyelash* . . . a part of *myself* that was doing me in.

* * *

Ah, so.
It seems to be ever thus. I am the cause of my own blindness, the source of my own sharpest hurts. And it is only when I get the distortions of *self* out of the way, that I can see at all clearly.

For this I pray: Dear Lord, lift me out of the blinding, inhibited narrow-mindedness of self-consciousness . . .

that I might see.
Amen.

Dear Lord,
It's three o'clock in the morning, a rare and special time that I have not observed in just this way before.

I haven't been tossing and turning—or losing sleep. I just happened to notice that I *was* awake, and that the still night was beautiful, and waiting for me. So I got up to enjoy this time of quite-awakeness.

I came out into the yard, just to stand here, feet bare . . . to savor the dark . . . to admire the stars . . . (there seem to be so many *more* of them to-night) . . . to indulge in aloneness . . . to worship quietly, without need of liturgy.

It's good, simply to be awake to the dark.
And awake to thee, in the dark.

I thank you, Lord God, for the peace of this early morn.

I shall sleep now, refreshed.
And wake, refreshed, remembering.

Amen.

I stole her limelight, Lord,
I pilfered her moment of glory.
And it was grossly unjust.
I've *had* my moments of glory.
But she's young. Playing the ingenue. New to the limelight—
a little unsure of her cues—
a little ill at ease as to how the world will receive her.
She started a story.
Her entrance was graceful—
and then I butted in,
and stole her limelight.
Father, forgive.
Forgive my blundering insensitivity.
Forgive my presumptious taking over by the sheer force of my adulthood.
In doing so, I incapacitate, overwhelm, undermine her—
and render her speechless.
I leave her floundering in her own helplessness.
It could have been a valid moment for her—
but I stole it.
Forgive.
And give me the insight to see it happening *before* it happens, next time.
Ah—give me the insight to retire to the audience when I see her on stage.
Amen.

Dear Lord,
That tree outside my window—
it's my neighbor's tree.
But by circumstance of geography . . . that is, of the location of my bed, and of my neighbor's tree . . . it is the first sight I see every morning, and the last, silhouetted by moonlight, every night.
In summer, it's green shade whispers through my open window.
In winter, it makes delicate and gently moving lace against the sky.
Thank you, God,
and thank you, neighbor,
for the many-splendored pattern of tree,
outside my window.

Amen.

Dear Lord,
He leaves home today.
starting out on life outside the walls of our home,
outside the protection of our watchful care.
        And I'm not ready.
This day has been coming . . . slowly . . . for these eighteen years—but suddenly it's here. There will be one less place to set at the table.—There will be no reason to doze lightly until he comes in at night—no need to check his dirty clothes hamper.
        And I'm not ready to let him go.
Life will never be the same again for him. Even when he's home for vacation times, it won't be the same.
  He'll never really be our little boy again.
        And I'm not ready to let him go.
But, Lord, this is what we wanted for him. This is what we have worked toward for eighteen years—
  that he might be able to cope,
  able to move out with maturity in his *own* sphere,
  able to *be* his own personality,
    and live out his own possibilities.
Help me remember, through my tears and anxieties
  how *ready* he is to go—
  how at home in your world he really is—
  how sensitive he has become to people, to needs,
    . . . to you.
I am grateful, Lord,
  grateful that this one steps out in faith.

Amen.

Ah, Lord,

The *ant* in me has just put up seventeen quarts of green beans. Now the grasshopper in me can fiddle away the rest of a summer's afternoon with a clear conscience.

And I suppose it's the puritan ethic in me that puts it this way—insisting that fun times be earned . . . merited . . . justified!

Why so? Sometimes the play-time is just as needful, and valid, and . . . well, *justified* as the work.

But we are hard taskmasters with ourselves—making long lists of "have-tos," that don't even mention the fiddling.

Lord . . . have I got into such a *habit* of "having-to" that I am not even aware of my *need* to fiddle?

Time-study experts insist that people work better when they take breaks from the routine.

Me, too?

Ah, yes! There *is* a new lilt to my chores when I take a moment off—when I stop—and stretch—and sing—when I think my own thoughts for a minute—rejoice in life for a minute—allow the grasshopper in me to fiddle his time without interruption.

The *alternation* makes the return to the task (or the lists) so much more palatable.

Let me permit myself these moments.
Let me include them in my list,
acknowledge their validity—
and spice my days with playfulness.

Amen.

Dear Lord,

When he held up that little sign, hastily lettered on a piece of notebook paper with a bright pink marking pen:

KINDNESS
Spoken Here

I cringed, for I had just handled a minor infraction of domestic rules in a rather devastating manner.

Then he smiled, to let me know it was still okay between us. And that made it possible for me to smile, too, somewhat ruefully.

I borrowed his sign, though, to hang over my desk, in case it might help me next time, *before* the devastation.

Thank you, God, for this openness between us—that he *can* call me to task when I need it.

And forgive me for the way in which I save my unkindnesses for those I love the most.

I observe certain courtesies with my neighbor's kids, and then throw barbed remarks at my own.

Kindness spoken here? Ah, Lord, let it be so.
Let the necessary disciplines be spoken in love.
Let the certain courtesies apply to my own.

I need not be a linguist to remember to use the language of love.

Amen.

Ah, Lord,

I have seen a beautiful thing.

They have a child who will remain a child, all his life. *And they give thanks for him,* and celebrate his membership in their family. The love and the acceptance all the others in the family hold for him is beautiful indeed. But then, as if that weren't enough, there is this *delight* they have in him.

It's a bonus, I guess—*because* of the love, and because of the open and honest acceptance. These have made them free to enjoy this youngest one—free to laugh with him as he discovers new wonders in his world—free to celebrate with him each achievement—free to enjoy *his* love, his uniqueness.

Ah, Lord—to *enjoy* his uniqueness! I have seen a beautiful thing.

> Is it because they *trusted* you, that they knew their situation had within it the possibilities for growth and love for *all* the family? Is it because they *continue* to trust you that they *continue* to rejoice in this child—without reserve, without "if onlys"? Ah, Lord, they have been blessed—richly blessed—and they have become, in the process, a blessing.

I have seen a beautiful thing.

Amen.

Lord,
So many of my young friends seem to be choosing childlessness as their life-style.
I'm glad they have the option, because an unwanted child is, and has, an awesome burden. But I wish there were some way to tell them how much fun it's been . . . and continues to be . . . to *have* children.
I watch them grow—I grow *with* them—gaining new insights of my own as I see the world through their wide-open eyes.
I see them reach out to new interests, and find *my* horizons broadened, *my* world enriched.
I watch them become people, and sense that I, too, am still in the process of becoming!
I share their laughter and their love and find the days of my life made lively and rich.
In trying to reveal the wonders of your world to them, I have found them newly revealed to me.
And Lord . . . how can I say this . . .
in trying to understand and cope with the awesome responsibilities of being a parent, I have come to a closer (and humbling) . . . and different . . . understanding of you.

My children have added heights and depths—(Ah, yes—and sleepless nights)—and joys and wonder and beauty and excitement to my life. I wish I could tell them.

Thank you, Lord.

Amen.

It was a beautiful morning, Lord,
but she nagged it to shreds.
Nagged because things were as they were,
and not as they might have been . . .
and nagged at the rest of us for existing at all.

* * *

I do that, too, Lord,
but I don't notice it so much.
I'm *appalled* at the way *she* can devastate us all with her tongue.
But I don't really realize what's happening when *I* do the devastating.
Besides, *I have the right.*
These are my children,
and I've got to bring them up right.
Father, forgive.
These are thy children—
It is my responsibility to guide them—
and to provide them with the security of a disciplined parent—

but not ever to nag their mornings to shreds.

Let me hear clearly
what my tongue is doing
—and desist.
Amen.

For thou art with me—
For you are near—
Thou—you—

Ah, Lord. I get almost hung up, sometimes, on the Cosmic Pronoun . . . almost.

Sometimes you *are* you, and I mull over my problems in your presence—grateful that I can be . . . *comfortable* . . . in your presence, and that I *can* come to you as Father . . . and as friend.

And other times I am aware—dimly, *awe*fully aware of the Mystery of thy presence—aware of a Nature that cannot be reduced to the knowable—and in reverence and humility I pray "Thou."

Nor is there any conflict. For words are not the ultimate prayer, in either case—they are merely my way of groping for thee. It is only *I* who am confined to mortal rhetoric.

You—Thou—
Ah yes, let my prayers be always so—
for I would not want to lose the awareness either of the approachable and loving Father to whom I come—or of the Mystery, before whom I worship.
For Thou art with me—
and You are near.
Let me be daily more aware that both are true.
Amen, Amen.

Well, Lord—

I have been led to worship . . . by a bug. It has happened before, for cicadas have co-existed with me for some years.

But last night was close-up.

Lord . . . he's such an *ugly* thing, crawling out of his earthen dungeon after thirteen years of exile, crawling *straight* for the nearest tree . . . and up it, to rest a moment . . . and then to split the ugly cretinous husk, and emerge—all new. All wet, yet, and deformed by the dampness of the larval womb . . . but patient—waiting to stretch and dry the wilted-lettuce stumps of wing until they become taut, firm lace—to bear him wherever he would go.

He's singing now, outside the window.
And I am singing, too—
inspired by a bug.

I give thanks, with deep joy,
that I have beheld this thing,
that I live in a world where such miracles keep happening.

Amen.

Lord, snatch me away from the comfort and security of a small and fist-held faith—for I find myself *seeking* comfort and security, when I should be seeking thee . . . when I should be seeking new and vaster concepts of thee.

My faith is a small and stunted thing.

I've kept it safe, and secure—

my size.

Not *your* size.

I have been unwilling to look beyond the downy nest of my contentedness—unwilling to risk.

I still am, and I'm horrified . . . and thrilled . . . at the very thought of grappling with a larger faith.

Ah, Lord! What *do* you have in store for me?

What heights . . . and depths of faith lie out ahead?

I cannot know until I'm willing to move out from the cozy,

into the unknown. So—

tear me away from my security.

Thrust me forward into the unknown

for *you* will be there.

And that is all the security that I shall need.

Amen.

Dear Lord,

This is not my time of prayer—
and I'm not praying—
I'm just writing a check.

But the check I'm writing is to the church, and I don't know what to put in that lower left hand "what for" space.

I can't put "tithe," for this isn't a tenth, and it seems a singularly inappropriate thing to *lie* about.

I won't put "gift," for that seems . . . presumptuous . . . as though I were the Lady Bountiful, graciously offering a small token of my plenty. It's as validly a "debt" as a "gift." Maybe more so.

What it's *for* is light bills and literature, and a little bit of outreach.

What it's *for* is partial payment (and I shall never be able to make payment in full) for what the church has done in helping me raise my family . . . in helping me keep my own priorities sorted out . . . in helping me tune in again to thy evernearness.

I shall put . . . "on account" . . .
and this *is* a prayer,
and the prayer that it is,
is thanksgiving.

Amen.

Dear Lord,
My soul is run down at the heels,
and the spring that was in my step has lost its savor.
My metaphors all come out mixed,
and my mind reneges at the thought of sorting them out.
So I shan't.
There really is no need for sorting them out.
I know how I feel,
and *you* know how I feel—
that's why I'm here . . .

Accept me thus, Lord, unsprung and undone.
Befriend and comfort me, and lead me for awhile by the hand. Like a child.
Like the little child that I am, sometimes.
Before thee, I recognize my immaturity. And confess it.
Before thee, I discover that I find no comfort in it—
for childishness no longer fits.
Before thee, I find reconfirmation of my selfhood.
And, comforted, I am enabled to stand alone,
and to step forward renewed, *savoring* the perspectives that adulthood makes possible.
Amen.

God, forgive.

He was hovering—
  and I was trying to think . . .
  trying to press on to the idea that balanced precariously on the edge of my consciousness . . .
and I told him to buzz off.

Nicely, of course.
Nicely, and not in so many words—
  but that's what I told him.
  And he got the message.
  Now he's gone. And so's the idea . . .

It had to do with love—
and with being sensitive to the
  unspoken needs of another.

Ah, Lord, forgive.
I have a deafness to expiate.

Ah, Lord,
I am grateful that I am free to doubt. It has not always been so.
I remember the years when I clutched my faith tight in my fist—unwilling to loose my hold on it for a moment of examination . . . lest, when I peeked, I might find it not there.
And the clutching kept it small—containable—and I carried it around as a talisman, to keep me safe.
And I *suspected* that what I clutched might be *only* a talisman . . . which made me *more* afraid to look.
But, ah, Lord, whose love enfolds me—
whose care has ever exceeded my capacity to comprehend it . . .
it is your love that forced me to unfold my hand —to be open to the doubts that troubled me.
So I looked, because ultimately I *had* to look . . .
and found that the doubts were small . . . petty little niggling things trying to confine a faith that needed only the *space* to grow. The faith was of thee.
My little doubts could not really reduce it to a fist-full.
Only I had to look beyond my doubt-troubled faith in *faith,* before I could be sure of a faith in *thee.*
Ah, Lord . . . is this a part of my humanness—
a part of the rhythm of life—
that I *still* find myself alternately clutching at a faith-too-small and rejoicing in the wondering assurance of a faith-unmeasurable?
I come now, hands open—rejoicing.
Bless with thy assurance tomorrow's doubts—even as you bless this moment's certainties.
Amen.

Ah, Lord, you ask hard things.
Love thy neighbor . . .

and I don't recall any escape-clauses about a "neighbor" who happens to be so *dreadfully* unlovable.

You know the one I mean.

Love her?

I've tried. But her comments are acid, barbed. Her ways are devious and hostile. And I come away seething. Or licking my wounds.

I've even tried again, tried for a loving smile, tried approaching with some small gift of self . . .

which she belittles, or repudiates—and that leaves me licking my wounds again.

Simply love her?

It isn't so *simple,* Lord. She *resists* loving. She denounces my proferred tokens, and takes pot shots at my selfhood. But I know it's a lonely fortress from which she looks out . . . on an alien world . . . and so, eventually, I *try* again.

And get the same result again.

Ah, so. Help me accept this, Lord—that she may continue to turn away, and to turn me away. That's her privilege.

But let me remain open to the possibility of friendship . . . some day, in case she should ever wish it.

Let me remain open to the possibility.

Amen.

Dear Lord, forgive.

I spend a good bit of time spinning my wheels—
looking for things that aren't really lost—
or standing in another room, wondering what in
heaven's name I came into that room to get,
or to do—and having to go back to where
I was when I made the decision, to find out—
so I could *then* go back to the other room to
get it, or do it . . . spinning my wheels.

Part of the reason, I suppose, is because I'm *not* a good housekeeper. If I were I could *find* the things that aren't really lost. If I were, I might not even wander around vaguely so much.

And yet—sometimes being a good housekeeper is the absolute ultimate in wheel-spinning.

Ah, I shall not fret too much.

It has just taken me 2½ hours to do the supper dishes . . . because I stopped seven times to admire, with my youngest, the illustrations in a truly fascinating bug book . . . and three times to help the middle one decipher a shirt pattern . . . and once for an extended conversation with my eldest on his Hermann Hesse book.

And I did get the dishes washed.

So . . . it's okay.

I'm not sorry it took 2½ hours. I'm sorrier about the *other* times, when I've washed the dishes with oblivious efficiency . . . and thereby missed so much.

Keep me reminded, Lord, that I am not *by profession* a dishwasher—and that there are times when other things have priority.

Keep me free from *too much* efficiency. Keep me open to interruptions—open to the delightful opportunities of my dailiness.

And if a certain amount of wheel-spinning results, it's okay.
I shall not fret.

Thank you, Lord, God—
for this very nice day.

Dear Lord,
It has just occurred to me that I am somewhat past forty, and *nothing* works as well as it used to.
I don't see as well.
Or hear as well.
Or run as well.
I don't jump that little short fence like I used to . . . but walk sedately around by the driveway instead. Sometimes my joints ache, and I get a hitch in my getalong.
Or one of the kids says, "Let's . . ."
and I say, "Oh, let's not."
Because, at that moment, my exuberance is already spent.
But oh Lord, God!
The *benefits* I do enjoy! A new idea comes, and I have forty years worth of perspective from which to regard it! I see subtleties and flavors and colors that I would have missed before.
And the soul sings a richer, deeper, far more wondrous song than it has sung before.
I thank you, God, for the years of my life. . . . and I would not trade forty for twenty again . . .
atall atall.
Amen!

I have done it again, Lord . . .
boasted of my busy-ness,
as if being over-occupied,
or having a list longer, or more imperative than hers,
were a virtue.
Strange . . . my sense of the appropriate.
Stranger still, my concept of what's valid.

Lord, I ask forgiveness not only for my boasting,
but also for my lists—
for my much-ado—
for the over-preoccupation that, on some days,
shackles my very soul.
Today, let me simply *do* the things that must be done,
without fanfare or numerical itemization—
and *then,* let me have the grace to hush—
let me have the courtesy to *deny* my friends the
tedium of a recital of my schedule—
lest it become an added burden to us both.
Amen.

Dear God,

I thank you for the deep and healing therapy of growing things.

When I was a child, I found it in a cottonwood tree—and I climbed high not only to escape *from* the real and heartless world, but to escape *to* a clean, fresh world, where green leaves whispered secrets in my ears, and cool breezes washed away the frustrations, and left my child-mind at rest.

I find that therapy still.

Climbing cottonwoods is no longer my style—but weeding the yard—or repotting the Swedish ivy—still brings me peace. I escape *from* the world of machines which always seem to be bossing me around. And I escape *to* a quiet and uncluttered time of awareness.

Maybe it's because the earth is my natural habitat, and getting close to it is renewing. I surrender myself to the *feel* of earth, of a leaf, of water, of a tree trunk or an old clay pot—and find it healing.

Ah, Lord, the earth is thine—
and I am thine—
and the healing is of thee.
For with thee is my natural habitat.
And in thee is my peace.

Amen.

Ah, Lord,
All we, like sheep . . .
oblivious of the world around us,
aware only of blundering other sheep in front of us . . . blundering ourselves . . .
stumbling into some shallow depression and regarding it as fatal, insurmountable, inescapable . . .
wrapped in woolen batting,
bleating out our insecurity.

How in need of a shepherd we are.
For we, like sheep, have gone astray.
I, like sheep.
And you, Lord, are my shepherd.
You supply my needs.
You find green pastures when I hunger,
and lead me to water when I thirst.
Even the awareness of my own mortality brings no alarm
—for you are near.
Ah, Lord, *that's* what matters.
That's what makes all the difference.
I lift my eyes above the woolly sea of other sheep around me, and *see* that you are near.
In thee do I put my trust.

Amen.

Lord,

It has been a week like none other I have ever known—and I wonder that I was ever reluctant to go. But a church camp for mentally retarded *adults* is an awesome thing to contemplate!

Ah, Lord—it *was* an awesome thing. Over and over I was struck with awe—with wonder—with humility—and delight. There were times . . . without number . . . that I had the feeling of standing on holy ground . . . of being with whole persons, so lately come from thee.

I am accustomed to living in a world where people wear masks—and there were no masks there—only openness to each moment—to each project—to each other soul present. No masks—no mists to shove aside—but real persons already revealed—open—vulnerable—and loving.

And I was struck with awe.

Ah Lord, I give thanks for the gift which they have bestowed upon me. Out of their child-likeness, they have given me the freedom to see things as they are . . . not having to figure them out, nor calculate their possible ramifications

but simply to *enjoy* them—
simply to *be* in the presence of the world—
and in loving fellowship with other people—
simply to be.
It *is* an awesome thing,
and I give thanks.

Amen.

Lord, what he said was,
"You can have instant coffee, and instant tea, and instant potatoes,
but you can't have instant relationships."
And he was right.
We can't measure out a portion of ourselves to each other, and stir once, and be friends.
Or measure out an instant prayer, and beat with a fork until fluffy.
For "instant" never quite satisfies like the real.
And a depth relationship has a mutual history of shared joy and anguish.
It is a mellowed blend of caring and being cared for—
of listening—
of removing masks (which is seldom easy)—
of openness and honesty . . .
without which no relationship is valid.
Not with him . . . nor with them . . . nor with thee.
All of this takes time. And effort.
And expenditure of self.
So, Lord, why do I keep asking for instant communion? Why am I not willing to put the same effort —the same care—into my relationship with thee, that I have found necessary in my relationships with others?
Why am I so unwilling to wait?
So unwilling to apprentice my soul?
So reluctant to do *my* part?
Ah, Lord. I come . . . in joys and in anguish . . .
in my moments of peace, and in my times of quiet desperation—

to sing,
to listen,
to pour out my humanness,
to remove my masks . . .

Amen.

Mostly, Lord, life is like a movie film.
The reels go by smoothly, quickly, in living color.
There is action in it, and plot—
lots of characters, major and minor—
and it holds the records of the seasons and the years.
But I thank you, Lord, for this wondrous power of recall, that lets me bring into focus a single square of the film,
and hold it still
and savor it again—
though it be a moment from the past.

I have such a picture of a sun-struck meadow,
incredibly green, and dotted with poppies.
Another, of a child's upturned face,
blissful, muddy—and mine.
And another, of a cherry tree in bloom,
and a purple finch sampling delicately of the blossoms—and I, like the bird, in tune with the universe.

Preserved images . . .
mental replays . . .
for these I give thanks.

Amen.

He's in our church choir . . .
and he wears a pair of faded and comfortable cut-off jeans under his choir robe.
And this says something to me.
about change—
and generations—
about feeling "at home" in the house of God—
about participation,
and lack of pretense (on his part . . .
and perhaps about *pretense* on mine.)
and it always makes me look at the church in a different light—as a living and vital "now" experience . . .
not as an archaic, cloistered, "in-group" ceremony.
He is not less devout, for his cut-offs—
and his singing in the choir is a freely given offering of himself.
He calls me to worship, somehow—and I'm glad I know that under his choir robe, *that* one, second from the left on the back row, sings his praise in faded and comfortable cut-offs.

Amen.

The *calling* that was mine, Lord,
the task in all the world that I felt *you* wanted me to do—has been denied me.
There is no way around it . . . nothing I can do to "fix" it.
Red-tape has ruled me no longer eligible
and the task that I delighted in,
that I felt so *right* about,
has been given to others.
And I hurt inside.
I hurt for the task, and for those whose lives were enriched by it.
And I hurt for myself.
I am bereft.
I am left *without* a task, without a calling—
and I hurt inside.
I have prayed "Use me, Lord,
or cast me aside . . ."
but I only meant the first part.
The second is almost more than I can bear.
Still, it has come to pass,
and bear it I must.
So . . . how does one adjust, Lord,
when one is left without a task?
Show me the way.
Show me your way . . .
to other tasks, other callings . . .
show me the way to see you, present,
in whatever work I do.
Help me see the possibilities,
and make it my calling,
and undertake it with the same enthusiasm

(Ah, Lord . . . that word again—
en-Theos . . . in-Thee-ness)
with the same enthusiasm
with which I tackled the other.

Amen.

Lord, I remember . . .
lemonade on the kitchen floor . . .
two gallons, I guess—pink—sticky—
and company due any minute.
And all because the punch bowl came unglued.
It was sitting there on the table,
just looking pretty and holding the lemonade.
And then . . .
it simply fell in two halves, and let the uncontained drink go where it would.
Which it did.

I could have panicked.
Might have . . . except that there wasn't time.
And besides, the rest of the family was already rallying, with towels, cuptowels, a mop, a pan of suds for the stickiness.
And it became, later, a delightful anecdote.

Dear Lord, I'm grateful for that perspective which time endows—a perspective that puts a mere two gallons of lemonade in its proper place . . . a perspective that separates the issues from the incidents, and saves the energy for the ones that *really* matter.

Help me keep this in mind. Amen.

It's okay.
I'm accepted.
I am accepted by the Lord of the Universe!
My past
my foibles
inconsistencies
self-debasements
pettinesses
and outright can't-call-'em-by-pretty-name sins
are accepted.
And that accumulated burden of guilt can be tossed in the trash.
I shan't be needing it any more.

I've known all this for a long while, Lord—
known that I was truly and totally accepted.
But once in awhile I forget—
and go scrabbling around in the trash can,
hunting for the old familiar guilt-burden I used to bear.
And then I remember.
I am accepted.
Unmasked,
sine cera.

Praise God!
Amen.

Lord,

Forgive me for trying to change the subject.

Just when the conversation begins to touch on something that *matters,* I shy off. I begin to feel uncomfortable, for fear I might not have something edifying to say—and so I speak instead of the weather (totally impersonal) or of gardens (usually a nice *safe* topic).

But she is dying. And *that's* what she wants to talk about. Her one death . . . and nobody will share it with her—nobody will be open enough and honest enough and free enough to *talk about something that matters.*

"Out of consideration for her," I don't mention it.

And "out of consideration for me," neither does she. And so we talk, pointlessly, of pointless things—and what could have been a deeply valid encounter, becomes a mutually uncomfortable effort to make conversation.

Forgive, Lord. She doesn't have *time* for small talk.

It happens at other times, too, Lord . . . that I am remiss.

My neighbor has a retarded brother—a great hulk of a man—for whom she cares as though he were three.

But *I* talk to her about the iris—

and the price of cheese.

How much we miss, she and I, by our unwillingness to talk about things that matter.

It isn't that I'm afraid to talk about such things, *once the initial confrontation* has taken place. But I shy away from bringing up the subject. I hesitate to speak the enabling word . . .

whether I'm the one who needs the help,
or whether I'm the one who might be in a
position to give it.

Father, forgive.

Forgive my withholding—
my reluctance to risk.

Amen.

It's been bonus—this last hour—this early-morning miscalculation of getting there at five instead of six. And I've had it all to myself—a whole hour of summer coolness

—the lovely dark

—the morning star

—and that little red-twinkling one down below it

—clouds, wandering across the sky, arranging themselves for a sunrise not yet come.

It's been a bonus.

Sometimes I don't know what to do with solitude—even when I can find some!

I wander around picking up things and putting them down again, as though I were not at ease with just myself.

And other times . . . ah, Lord, I give thanks for these blessed other times, when I can be wholly alone —and *whole,* alone.

Whole, with thee—as I am never complete *without* thee . . . and aware—

awake-to-life.

Only six o'clock? Ah! I've *already* had a good day—already *lived,* and been glad, rejoiced in an early morning's pristine loveliness.

Oh, let me remember . . .
because tomorrow morning, when I'm foggy with sleep, I'll forget *how* lovely,

and how renewing this time has been . . .

and my hand will hover indecisively

over the clock.

Amen.

Because he is mine,
  I weep when he goes astray.
Because he is yours,
  I pray.

Father, God . . . be with him.
  (I know that you are—
    but he does not know—
    nor wish to.)
Surround him with intimations of divine love—
haunt him with symbols of faith,
lure him,
  through the books he reads,
  the music he listens to,
  the thoughts that drift, unsought, through his head.
With thy Holy Spirit,
  that divine Presence present within us,
    entice him into caring.
      For the course he now wanders aimlessly
      leads nowhere.
Pursue him, Lord—
    until he finds thee.

Amen.

Dear Lord, *you* know.

Gracefulness is not in me. I stumble up stairs, and I clump down them. I am socially inept. I blurt before I think. I put my foot in my mouth—sometimes *both* feet—and then I get so self-conscious that I can't say anything at all.

And then I pity poor me, that I should have flubbed things again.

How come *I'm* such a dud? In a world full of strong, stable, *competent* people, I feel extremely insecure.

* * *

Lord, here I go again,
focusing too sharply on myself.
I forget that *other* people also feel insecure, struggle with doubts, wrestle with fears, labor over decisions.
Because I only see the things they *do,* I don't know anything about the inner turmoil they have to go through before they do them.
Strong, competent people?
Ah, Lord, we are *all* insecure.
We are all in need of thy grace.
Give us the strength to wrestle and to labor.
And give us the insight to recognize our common quandary.

Amen.

Ah, Lord,
It's scary,
changing careers at half past grown-up.
And he *feels* the fears, deep in his bones.
What if he invests a year—two—in going back to school—and then . . . when he's ready, nobody *wants* his skills?
What if the sacrifices involved *cost* too much?
Ah, Lord—no wonder he feels the fears.

But the beautiful part is that he's doing it anyway.
He's weighed the options,
and considered the possibilities, and the ramifications thereof . . .
and he has decided to take the necessary risk because of a divine call to serve the *secular* community.
And I am humbled, and heart-warmed,
to see him do it.
I've watched his fears grow less as a new sort of joy creeps into his eyes, his laugh, his step.
No wonder.
He has Cosmic Permission
to walk a new road.
God, go with him.
Amen.

In this one regard at least, I am like the disciples—
I have a tendency to shoo the children away.
Ah, Lord, how *slightly* I regard other people's children.
How prone I am to talk over their heads, and over their heads, to their parents . . . ignoring their presence and their humanness.
It's not that I regard them as unworthy—
it's just that so often I do not regard them at all.
And having shooed them away—
having eliminated them from my consciousness—
I proceed to talk to my peers about
Matters of Consequence.
And the children stand around, belittled.
Or wander off somewhere else in search of their identity.

Father, forgive my barbarism.
It is more than a rudeness—
it is a gross miscarriage of Christian love.
Of such as these is the kingdom of heaven . . .
and I, unperceiving, have missed out on their contribution to an understanding of what life is all about.

Forgive.
Amen.

Dear Lord,
I have, on occasion, prayed for the gift of tongues—for those who have that gift speak of the joys of praising thee in a spirit voice.
But I suspect that the *reason* that I have prayed for this is not that I might have the joy, but that I might have the *assurance*.
And tongues would be a Sign.

Ah, Lord—
if you would have me sing your praise in tongues as yet unknown to me,
let it be so.
And if not,
let it be so.
I am content. I shall not howl, like a thankless child, because the gift I receive is not the same as the gift my brother finds so valid.
For, as we were not all *reached* in the same way, so we are not all *endowed* in the same way—or *blessed* in the same way.
And I have been blessed.
I have the assurance of your present presence. There are times when awareness wells up within me, and my soul rejoices. And you honor the unspoken psalms I sing. And I am blessed. Amen.

Dear Lord,
I have been priested to by an uncommonly ordinary saint.
This second conversion of hers has been a strange experience, both for her to live out and for me to watch. *You* know . . . Lord, she has almost completed a forty-day fast.
This is . . . was . . . appalling to me. Nor would I, even now, undertake it.
And yet for her it has been valid.
And I, confronted, by her fast,
am confronted also with the knowledge
that there are things about which I know nothing.
She is undergoing a spiritual experience, and yet there is still this delightful *humanness* about her—
this readiness to chuckle—
this eagerness to bake bread, to minister to *another's* need—
this delight in continuing to cook for her family—
this delight in life.
I have not known anyone before who experienced such a second birth, who was so *non*judgmental about it, so gently humble, and so very real.
There is nothing other-worldly about her—for she is very much a part of life and of *this* world. And the messages she gets from you, Lord, are calls to simple service—basin and towel in hand.
I had always thought of *saints* as awesome, transparent, but somehow formidable creatures. And she's so . . . human . . . with a sense of humor that spices the lives of all around her.
Saint?

Perhaps.

Her fast has enriched *her* faith, I know—
And mine, as well. I know that, too.

Thank you, Lord,
for the earthy ministry
of such earthly saints.
Amen.

"I don't know why I even *come* to church," she muttered. "I never seem to get anything out of it anymore."

Ah, Lord, how strangely we distort things.
I've had that feeling, too . . . but I'm not sure *why*.
I do not go to visit my *friend* with that in mind. She does not come to see *me* so that I will give her roses; I have none. She does not come to borrow my books—for most of my books are on loan already, from the downtown library. Neither of us goes to *get anything*—except a certain communion that happens between friends.
Ah, Lord, this gets to be our hang-up . . . that we go to the church in a "what's-in-it-for-me" frame of mind, as if "getting something out of it" were our sole purpose in going.
How strangely we distort things!
Our purpose for going is to worship, corporately, which is something that even *profound* private worship neither duplicates nor replaces.

Ahh, Lord, we *do* get much out of it—not because of our deservings, but by thy grace—and as *by-products*.
The burden is not on thee, to *give* us our share, but on ourselves, to offer ourselves up to thee.
The purpose of our coming is to acknowledge our source, and to worship.
Let us not forget.
Amen.

Dear Lord,

I close my eyes . . . beseechingly . . . in prayer—for I am lonely, and can't seem to get through to you tonight.

I close my eyes . . . hoping for a sense of Presence. And what comes through is a sense of pattern—pieces of light and color kaleidoscoping past my still-closed eyes. And they bring me no peace at all. I find them interesting, but they are not what I'm looking for.

Are you avoiding me?

That scarcely seems in character, Lord.

You are always there—always available to me—always reaching out to me. So why should there be these times, when I can't get through?

Am *I* avoiding *you?*

I hadn't thought so.

And yet—I guess I have been seeking on *my* terms again—seeking the Divine Stamp of Approval on what I've already chosen to do, asking for security—for a nice, understandable agreement with you, that in exchange for my "being a good Christian," I shall receive a warm feeling in my gizzard.

Ah, Lord . . .

that's not what I want . . . a pat on the back is not my goal, nor is "instant security" that for which I long.

It is *thee* for which I long.

Oh, the unspeakable gall of me, that I should seek to make deals with Almighty God!

If the price of thy presence is *in*security, let it be so.

I come. That's all. I just come.

No bargains, no desperate *please* about "let's

do it my way." I just come.
I shall not avoid thee, Lord,
for it is thy presence I seek.
Lord, I believe.
Help thou my recurring unbelief.

Amen.

This is a dull, dead day, Lord,
and weariness hangs over me like a pall.
Please hold me excused: I cannot pray.

Ah, so.
I find it difficult to rise to the occasion of prayer, when my thoughts are cold and lifeless things.
I find it a little stilted to praise thy name, when lassitude benumbs my soul.
And yet—I cannot *not* pray.
I come.
I bring my weariness, and my . . . self-pity . . . and offer them as sacrifice. Only here, in thy presence, do I even recognize them for what they are. Only here do I realize how I cling to them. For if I mourn "Poor me!" with enough pathos, someone else may be sufficiently impressed to say, "Oh, yes! Poor you!" . . . which might be comforting.

Ah—a shallow hope of comfort, that.

God of grace and understanding, I relinquish my cherished inadequacies, and my carefully nurtured self-pity. This was not *created* to be a dull, dead day. It is only I who have made it so. And I repent of it. The comfort that I need, I find in thee . . . and the renewing strength.
This is a quiet and peaceful day, Lord, and there may be woven all manner of shining moments into it
—for those who are willing to perceive them. Let me be one.

Amen.

Ah, Lord,
On such a day I could let the "child" in me out to play. I could marvel at the smoothness of a stone, at the stellar symmetry in a slice of okra. I could take off my shoes, and wriggle my toes in the soft grass.

Or I could finish painting the bathroom, and get the mending done for once. Which is what I *ought* to do.

Ah, Lord . . . *ought.* There's the hang-up. The "child" in me has been so hemmed in by "oughts" that she almost never gets out to play anymore—almost forgets the delicious feel of grass, almost ceases to wonder at the ripple of legs on a millepede.

The morning is full of wonder, and the child in me tugs to romp in it. So she shall!

Yes—oh yes! The grass *does* feel good to bare feet—just as I remembered it!
And there is new beauty in everything when I see it with the curious *this*-moment vision of the "child" that is *still* within me.

I'm grateful, Lord—deeply grateful that the child is still present, still likes to do such things, and that there are moments when I can delight in your creation . . .

wiggling my toes in the grass,

and romping in your good green world.

Amen.

Dear Lord,
Maker of suns and moons and shining comets—
and maker of the good green earth . . .
I stand unshod on this small isolated vacation meadow, for it seems *holy* ground,
and I would keep it so.

* * *

Odd, but I seldom think of the *street* in front of my house as holy ground,
and I almost never stand unshod upon it.
I suppose it's because streets are paved with asphalt, and reek of heavy machinery and brawny laborers
—while meadows are soft with grass and sweet clover, dappled with buttercups.
And yet—the street is as surely yours as the meadow.
Man is your creation, and where men gather together in community, there is possibility for communion as well.

Ah, my street *should* be holy ground.
And I shall learn to regard it so.
The meadow seems holy . . . for I feel thy presence here.
The street . . . ah yes—let me remember that you are there, as well.
There, *more so,* for there is where the action is—
there is where your people build their dreams . . .
and live out their lives . . .
and it is holy ground.
Let me seek less often to escape it—
and more often to participate,
validly, in its communion.

Amen.

Dear Lord,

I should not be too shook-up, I suppose, if we were to discover that there really *are* Martians. Or Venutians. Or Spacelings of other designation. Nor should I have any reason to fear them. For you, who made us, and this planet earth upon which we ride, made Mars and Venus . . . and Sun and suns . . . and all that is, or was, or shall be. That being so, then it was you who created Martians and Venutians and other Spacelings, if there be any. And if you created them, then they, too, have a part to play in the divine scheme of things. It is not necessary that I know their part—ah, how dimly I sometimes understand my own!

All I really need to know is that you are . . . and I am . . . and my neighbor is.

I don't know just what the relationship might be, between Martians (*if* they be) and you, Lord. But I *do* know what the relationship can be between us earthlings and you. It *isn't,* always, but the fault is ours. The possibility is there. The opportunity . . . the option of sonship . . . oneship . . . the power to become.

Ah, the whole of this incredible universe cannot offer more than that!

Then sings my soul!

Lord, God creator of all worlds that are,
creator of the me that is,
and the me that I could become,
accept this prayer of gratitude.

When I consider the heavens, the suns and moons
and wheeling planets which you have ordained,
I *do* stand in awesome wonder.

The more so, that I should stand on this one planet,
and reach out to thee, Lord of all,
and find thee, reaching out to me.
This is the greatest wonder.
I hold it, like a treasure,
and sing it, like a yodeling note of joy,
out to the farthest corners of space,
that the Lord God of the Universe . . . knows my name.

Amen, Amen.

Ah, Lord,
It's spring. A meadowlark chortles the glory of God, and a daffodil showeth his handiwork. A hyacinth in the dentist's office smells like essence-of-springtime, and an almost-stranger in the elevator lights up with the warmth of a genuine smile.

Some days are just *like* this . . . sharper, clearer, more in focus. The same route I take *every* morning is suddenly new—is newly beautiful. The same people I see every day are suddenly real to me, suddenly dear to me.

And there is a jubilance about life . . . a thrill-to-the-fingertips just to be alive and awake, just to be here and now.

How come, Lord? How come some days are like this? Why this sudden welling-up-within-me of exultant joy? If I knew, perhaps I could preserve it. Perhaps I could rejoice like this in *every* day.

Ah, you are wise. I couldn't stand this jubilance every day. And even if I could, it might become ordinary, until I might not even notice it.
But oh, *this* jubilant day!

I thank you, God, for this incredible, azure-blue day, which speaks to me repeatedly of your love.

I exult in it *now,* awake to its beauty, awake to the fellow-conspirators I meet. I exult in it now, and I shall savor its memory on many a later, ordinary day.

Amen.

Dear Lord,
their Europe slides were lovely—Michelangelo's *David*—Saint Paul's Cathedral—
evidences of man's traditional faith in you.
But there was that other slide of the nameless little roadside shrine on an incredible hill in southern Germany . . . just a stone alcove, with a statue of your Son, and on the table before it, six bowls of flowers . . . evidences of man's present faith. Crockery bowls, most of them—not new. Not matching. Nor were the flowers from the same garden.
My friends spoke of other evidences—
of the sound of church bells, tolling the Angelus . . . or matins . . . or pealing forth jubilant carillon calls to a service of worship.
They spoke of entering a little town in Holland, to find it virtually deserted on a Saturday evening, until the church doors opened at the end of a service, and the streets were suddenly *full* of folk.
They spoke of greetings passed, "in the name of God," . . . and of a tourist, like themselves, going into a church to gawk, and staying to worship.
And over and over they mentioned the church bells.

Faith of our Brothers, living still. Ah, Lord—how good it is to live in a world peopled at least in part by men and women of faith! Sometimes that faith is expressed in ways new and unfamiliar to me, for I don't put a vase of flowers at a roadside shrine to speak my love. But others did. And for this I give thanks.

I rejoice in these evidences of a *present* faith, a faith of our brothers, living still, here as well as over there—in spite of inflation, or loneliness, or the haunting shadows of futureshock. Faith of our brothers, who rejoice in your presence, and who recognize you as Father Almighty, whose mercy is over all his works, and whose will is ever directed to his children's good.

Amen, Amen.

Dear Lord,
Creator of all things—
I am compelled by that admission to regard *all things* as created by you—
and thus impelled to regard every blessed thing as a . . . *blessed* thing.
Hmm. This changes my perspective.
I find myself *tuning in* to things—
to the grape I eat . . .
conscious of vine and soil, sun and rain and harvest . . .
conscious in a new way of how delicious the taste really is . . .
appreciative, as I have not been before, of a grape as . . . a *gift*.
I find myself tuning in to the cloth I cut,
to the lawn I weed,
to the water I drink, or the tree I touch.
Ah, Lord, sometimes I am confronted with the whole of life—and I *see* it whole, and splendid . . .
and sometimes I find myself—like this—aware anew of some small part of the whole—aware of the wonder of this small part . . . this "blessed thing" —and thereby newly aware of the wonder of the whole.
How can I begin to give thanks—
that I was born into such a world . . .
and that, on occasion, I can *see* it thus!
Amen.

Dear Lord,

I thank you for the little idiocies that brighten my days.

Like the little old lady in the theater ticket box last night, who was *ironing* the dollar bills, so they'd be flat and neat and uncrumpled for her patrons. And who grinned, sheepishly, when we caught her at it.

And the blue jay who takes his morning shower in my sprinkler . . . leaning one shoulder into the spray—and preening, afterwards, oblivious of his audience of one.

I thank you for the spontaneity that *each* day is, and has—for the fresh and never-before-ness that add such verve to living.

I thank you for the little joys, for the unpredictable delights that put my solemn lists and plans into perspective.

Amen.

Dear Lord,
I come before you sometimes
with such piddling little prayers—
such idiocies—
that it is no wonder I go away unsatisfied.
When I am dishonest,
and try to hide from my own admission the things that really tear me up,
praying instead over "safe" little mundane topics . . .
well . . . I have not prayed.
I have merely given the rote prayer wheel of my inattentive mind a half-hearted turn.
You know the things that tear me up—for I *have* prayed over them before, sweat and hurt and agonized over them before.
What I have *not* done is let them go.

Dear Lord, I have done all that I can think of to do to resolve these problems. I bring them once again to you.
But this time, I shall *leave* them with you . . .
knowing that your love for those I love is deeper even than my own . . .
knowing that your grace is sufficient,
both for them, and for me.
I pray. I offer up this burden. And I leave it here with you.

Amen. Amen.

Ah, Lord . . .
This is the peace that passeth understanding . . .
to have left one's burdens with you.
Nothing is changed, but everything, *everything* is different.
Because of your sufficient grace and sustaining love,
I have been *enabled* to leave a couple of heavy and encumbering burdens.
It's not that in doing so everything has been magically solved . . . ZAP . . . for the facts of the case are still the facts.
But confessing those facts, and exploring them, in depth, in your presence—alters things!
Values change—and perspectives—and significance . . . until all is "wholly realigned . . ."

Ah, Lord, why did I not relinquish my clutch-tight hold on my private wrestlings long before now?
Small is my faith, and feeble my trust.
You have sustained me in the past—
but seems like it has to be a new struggle every time to let go the *real* burdens.
I give thanks . . . for divine patience
. . . for new perspective
. . . and for your wondrous peace,
which passes all understanding.
Amen.

Dear Lord,
I keep wondering about Enoch.
I wish we had some more biographical data about him. Because of all thy saints, he is the one I most would emulate.

For Enoch walked with you.

"Enoch walked with God," it says.

He had a family, Enoch did—sons and daughters.
Hmm. And he walked with you, I suppose,
with a two-year-old tugging at his cloak—
with a wife to provide for—
and with a payment due on the family dwelling?
Or did he have a patron who took care of the petty, nagging little things like the price of goat cheese and carob beans, so that he might be freed to devote himself to things of the spirit?

Seems unlikely.

We don't know much about Enoch—
just that he walked with you.

Permit me that quality of devotion that *whatever* the distractions, I might still be able to walk with you.

Amen.

Father, I thank you for this growing-up child of mine!
How nice it is, to get glimpses now and then of the kind of woman that she is becoming.
I like what I see. I like the gentle reserve with which she is feeling her way into adulthood . . . fairly cautiously . . . making little forays out into the grown world . . . withdrawing, when it seems too much . . . but beginning to be *at home* in it.
I like the way she retains a delight in *child* things —playing with the little kids who seek her friendship, going barefooted, regarding small creatures with tenderness.
She is steadier now than last year . . . less moody . . .more *fun* to have around . . . more responsible.
I don't often see her being selfish, but I do see her liking herself. I thank you for this. It displays a maturity that *I* did not come by for twice her years.
I give thanks for her . . .
for what she has meant
and does mean
and shall mean
to me.

Amen. Amen.

Lord,

I usually forget to give thanks for the miracle of my own body—capable of recreating its own cells to remain strong and useful to me, even after these years of wear and tear—

capable of mending itself, when I have rent or skint or burned or scratched it—

capable, as it has been, of receiving the seed and nourishing the cells that have become new bodies —and of giving them birth—

capable as it is of movement—of work—of coordination—of responding with new vigor to exercise and sleep, sunshine and fuel food.

I thank you, God, for breath and strength and energy—and for the feeling of aliveness within me. I thank you for the incredible continuing miracle of my own body.

Amen.

Dear Lord,
I drive the streamlined highway in my little car, and I am open to the unfolding view.
And I am grateful for the uninterrupted miles. They give me time to bask in my own unhurried reflections . . . time to talk, or to companionably *not* talk, with my family . . . time to just *be*.
And I am grateful.

The road is new, but the way is old, here.
Conquistadores strode these valleys. Priests of Old Spain walked beside them. Ah, little did they dream, even in all their dreamings, of the changes the centuries would bring.
Of covered wagons they may have dreamed—
and of homesteaders—
and even of villages which would come to be.
But not of superhighways which weave and cloverleaf to avoid the skyscrape cities into which the villages have grown.

I am grateful, Lord, for all that—
and for all this.
I cherish my roots—
and I cherish my rootlessness.
I drive the streamlined highway in my little car, and I give thanks to thee, God of times, and time, and all timelessness.

Amen.

Dear Lord,

It's no wonder we feel a little schizophrenic sometimes . . . for we allow ourselves to be cast in two roles—both as the puppeteer and the puppet.

Sad, that, for the puppeteer in us can live only vicariously, pulling the strings of the "image" he wants the world to see, pretending not to be there at all; pretending that the puppet is real. He can never quite summon the courage to come on stage himself. Life gets pretty tasteless, secondhand.

And all the time the puppet in us is indescribably bored, repeating someone else's lines, wishing he could cut the strings and be his own man.

No wonder life loses its savor!

Give us eyes to see what we are doing to ourselves, Lord. Give us the inner calm to be at home in the world—honestly, personally, at home—in the world.

Amen.

Dear Lord,

I was determined to make it up this hill without getting off the bike to push. But the hill was long . . . and every curve I rounded revealed another curve farther off and higher up. The breathing was hard, and the pushing was hard—but the rhythm of the wheels called the cadence, and the view going by made music for the eyes!

So . . . I made it! And here at the top I pause—for a long look, and a quick swig of water, and a prayer of thanksgiving.

Ah, a prayer of exultation is more like it—that I have been blessed with heart and lungs and legs strong enough to carry that part of me that sees and thinks and feels—and exults—through the days of my life!

Amen!

It was a neat little notebook, Lord.
I almost bought it.
Across the front it said

DUMB THINGS
I GOTTA DO

And that struck a responsive chord . . .
for a minute.
Then the chord became dissonant,
and I put the notebook down.
The reason . . . which I only tumbled to afterwards . . . is that the things I gotta do—*aren't dumb.*
I gotta pick up some groceries,
and mend the tile around the bathtub faucets. And get one kid some #2½ bass clarinet reeds, and another kid's gym suit washed, and another kid's blouse finished. And I have letters to write to the other two, and to a couple of long-time friends.
There's a book I need to read, because of what I think it says—and a letter I need to write, because of something that needs saying. That's besides going to work and coming home and all that.

But it's *my* list, Lord! It's *my* life-style. And it's not *dumb* stuff I gotta do.

I get it all wrong when I think I've got to get all the "things I gotta do" done, so then I can live. If I can't live *while I'm doing them,* then I better take another look at my perspectives.

Ah, Lord, bless with thy presence my day. The "things I gotta do" are mostly things that create "family" and "community." I'm grateful for my list.

Lord, bless with thy presence my day.

Amen.

Lord, a single parent has some lonely moments.
I've noticed this, in these almost-eight years of single-parenthood.
There are lonely moments of joy, that ache to be shared, and lonely moments of anxiety, which sharing might alleviate.
(But one does not waken a child, or summon a neighbor, at 2:00 A.M., to say . . . "Uh . . . would you come worry with me, for a little while?" Particularly if the worries are vague and blurry phantoms.)

But Lord, my *commonest* lonely moments involve the decisions I have to make, by myself.
Do I really need to call the plumber?
Did the hail damage the roof?
What shall we—ah, *I*—get . . . for her birthday present?
What shall I do about—how can I *possibly*—buy a car? . . .
I'd like so much not to have to *decide* things all the time.

Ah—not to have to decide. Is *that* my hang-up? It isn't the aloneness that bugs me, but it's the decision-making?
Well—if this is what it is, then why don't I quit blubbering and get on with it. A decision is easier *made* than muddled over.
And I am *not* alone.
There are decisions I can make by myself. I'll make those, and get them out of the way.
As for the other, harder ones—

I come before your presence, Lord,
there to look at them,
there to examine them,
there to decide.

For you are with me. Your rod and your staff do comfort me. You are my strength. Amen.

Absolve them from guilt, dear Father, if they should ever have to make the decision to "unhook the machines" and permit me to die my own death.
Let them *know,* deeply, that I would want it so.
Let them know that I have no fear of death, for my times are in thy hands, and I want to live out *all* the experiences of my life,
including that one.
For there comes a moment when a dying person *needs* death, as a sleepy person *needs* sleep. When that moment comes for me, let them have the strength and certainty to grant me my death.
And absolve them from guilt, Father. Let no burden of doubt or self-accusation remain with them, when I go home.

Amen.

Lord,
Three of them, all searching for careers—
all wondering where to invest—
and how to spend—
their lives—
weighing, considering.
But they seem less mercenary, in their considerations, than *we* were at 20—less concerned with "how much will I make?" "how much will it get me?" I am grateful.
I hear them asking, instead, "what kind of a *life* would it be?" . . . "how would I *feel* about doing that" . . . and even, occasionally, "would it make the world a better place to live in?"
And I am grateful.
Grateful that they sense already what it has taken my generation so long to learn . . . that profits, like pornography, are obscene, when they have no redeeming social values.
They've come a long way, it seems to me.
And I'm grateful.
Bless them, Lord, and bless the choices they make.
Amen.

Dear God,

Sometimes when I pray, one of me seems to stand to the side, and watch the other one of me in the act of praying. And the prayer itself is a rote and mechanical offering of proper little phrases—without life or light.

But other times, I am united within myself and with thee. And in prayer I mount up with wings as eagles.

I thank you, Lord God of all,
for these other times.

Amen.

Dear Lord, I've been thinking . . .

sometimes when I do *lots* of things, one of me seems to stand aside and watch the other one of me perform.

I watch myself being Gracious Hostess . . .
Efficient Manager . . . Good Mother.

I see me going through the motions that match the role. (*Proper* motions, like a trained pet, on cue.)

And it's like *I'm* not really involved. The *real* me is the one standing back watching, while the well-trained other me goes through the ritual of proper things to do.

But I'm not really involved.

And that creates an impersonal situation . . . an un-*human*-ness . . . that is rather bleak. It reduces what could have been a valid encounter to an automatic exchange of proprieties. By denying my uniqueness, by failing to be personally present, I have prevented what might have been good. And what might have been growth.

Father, forgive.

Help me get back together, and be a whole, and *caring,* person.

Amen.

•

Dear Lord,
"All you gotta do is cope," she said.
And I did.
Partly because there was no one else there to do it for me. I *had* to cope.
So I did.

And it was a good feeling.
There was real satisfaction in seeing that I *could* do the necessary deed. *Little* deeds, most of them.
Getting antifreeze in the car in time.
Replacing a light switch.
Putting new weather stripping on the front door.
Balancing the budget.
Lord, *you* know these aren't always the little things they sound like. Replacing a light switch, when I've never done it before, and when all I can think about is volts and watts and what if I get it wired up wrong—
and replacing weather strpping when I didn't even know what to call it at the hardware store—
and balancing the budget when it *won't* . . . not because I added wrong, but because the money simply isn't *there*
and then—the harder ones—
like making decisions that aren't really clear . . .
and expediting schedules for the whole tribe . . .
and calling myself to be present when my child needs to talk (difficult when it comes at a moment when I want only to be present to *myself*, off *by* myself, licking my own wounds.)
Still little things, Lord, but not always *easy* things.

I thank you for those times when I *can* cope.
I thank you for the feeling of worth-ness that comes when I have.
And I pray for those times that lie ahead—when I will need renewed strength and real insight to do the the necessary deeds.

Grant me most of all, Lord, a sense of your presence, as I live out my days.

Amen.

Thank you for night,
for rest when my body is too tired to move,
when my mind is too weary to think,
when my heart is too heavy to cope.
It's been a long, long day.
I have watched a friend make the agonizing decision to take her child off a breathing machine.
I have watched a child struggle to keep back the tears when a task was too difficult.
I have given all my energies to the children at school—and found my own family needing me when I got home.
And I've been lonesome and homesick for an absent loved one.
But it's nighttime.
Thank you for night,
for rest
when my body is too tired to move,
when my mind is too weary to think,
when my heart is too heavy to cope.
I leave it all in your keeping.

Amen.

What a delightful, terrible, awe-ful, wonderful task is mine!
Blessed little scamps!
Vulnerable,
Open,
Free,
Honest,
Searching,
Growing,
Creative,
Accepting,
And I am their teacher.
Don't let me blow it, God.
Don't let me stifle their pleasure in life about them.
Don't let me turn them off to trust and openness.

Ah, Lord—*bless* my little scamps—
and me, Lord—and me.

Amen.

All summer I'd hoped for rain—
fussed about the dry land,
complained about the heat, Lord.
Finally, it *did* rain!
and it rained—
and rained—
and rained . . .
And I hoped for sunshine—
fussed about the soggy earth,
complained about the damp chill,
Until
my daughter, with wonder in her voice, looked on the dirty-watered street and said, "How beautiful the colors are!" and there in an oil-leak spot, saw loveliness.

In the most unlikely place, Lord—
and in the midst of my most unlikely frame of mind.
I, mulligrubbing and discontent—
she, open to the beauty that lies, somehow, somewhere, all around us—
even in the most unlikely places.
Ah, I thank you, Lord, for this unlikely world!
When I am willing to see, there are such *neat* little wonders to behold!

Amen.

Lord, the choir has just sung my prayer—
and the haunting tune plays around the edges of my mind as I pray again, for myself, the equally haunting words:

"O Lord, how can we know Thee?
Where can we find Thee?
Thou art as close to us as breathing,
and yet art farther than the farthermost star.
Lord, how can we know Thee?
Where can we find Thee?
Thou art as mysterious as the
vast solitudes of the night
And yet art as familiar to us
as the light of the sun.
O Lord, how can we know Thee?
Where can we find Thee?

When justice burns like a flaming fire,
When love evokes willing sacrifice,
do we not bow down to Thee?
Thou livest within our hearts
as Thou dost pervade the world,
And we through thy presence behold."

Amen.

I saw it, Lord, that flower in a crannied wall that Tennyson talked about. Mine was a fleabane daisy, stretching up out of the thin crack of a cranny in a solid basalt cliff.

Ah, "*if* I could understand
What you are, root and all, and all in all,
I should know what God and man is."

I stood looking at it for a long while, Lord, pondering the imponderables.
And it seemed a clue—
one of many—
left here for us to ponder . . .
hints of *thy* nature . . .
in nature . . .
intimations of immortality . . .
in a mortal, cliff-clinging daisy—
and in a mortal, time-spanned mind.
Ah, Lord! For these blessed hints, these curious clues, we give thanks.

Amen.

Dear Lord,

I speak of clues—little lovely things that point me to thee . . .

But the real clue—the real *revelation* of "what God and man is" . . . is the man Jesus . . . who *showed* us what you are while he was showing us what we could become.

I seem to think more often in terms of thee, Lord . . . or of thy Holy Spirit, which is for me the Presence present . . . and less often of Jesus—man of Galilee, walking ordinary dirt roads and fishing in ordinary waters—a man who got hungry, and mad, who wept and laughed and agonized—who struggled with too many people and too little time and too much—*too* much to be done—and with deep, bone-weariness. And who managed somehow to come through—to put it all together into a meaningful, positive whole—into an *interpretation* of divinity in daily living.

I really prefer thinking about the Holy Spirit. That asks less of me. The Holy Spirit is not an *example* I feel called upon to follow.

But *Jesus?*

The *man?*

The *daily* interpretation of Emmanuel?

Ah, Lord . . .
this is thy clue!

Father,

Some days I feel that my mind has been bludgeoned by slogans—

on radios, on billboards, on posters, in songs —neat, pat slogans with neat, pat answers—
as though life were like that . . . all solved, and with no loose ends dangling.

And life *isn't* like that. Scarcely any situation is so simple that it can be summed up and dismissed in three words.

So why do *I* do it, Lord? Why do I resort to conversational "slogans"—as pat, and as superficial as the commercial ones? My child . . . or my friend . . . or an almost-stranger begins to tell of a problem—complex, as problems almost always are. She/he doesn't want my pat answer. What's wanted is my listening ear—and an atmosphere of acceptance in which her talking-through of the problem might lead to a deeper understanding. But when I toss in the slogan, the serious consideration skids to a halt. The slogan becomes a squelch . . . and she, deflated, talks instead of other things.

Forgive.
Forgive my egotistical need to "have the answers."
Forgive my feeling that other people's problems are simple ones that *can* be pat-answered—that only mine are real enigmas.
Forgive my insensitivity.

Amen.

Dear God,

The lesson said something about "taking stock of my own assets and liabilities." It was asking for *personal* assets and liabilities—not financial ones.

How much easier to fill out a financial sheet! For I've been taught that it is vain—wrong—to admit to my gifts.

What false modesty is that that makes me see myself as less than I am?

For I do.

I exaggerate my *un*gifts—tediously reviewing the goofs I make—and thereby prove to myself that I really *am* as unworthy as I thought I was.

And then I minimize my gifts. I never really re-examine the things I do *right*—never really even think about having *done* anything right!

And I certainly never take stock of myself, and deliberately plan my life with my assets and possibilities in mind!

Father, help me recognize my gifts—and teach my children to recognize theirs.

Remind me again that I am *your* creation, and let me rejoice in these my gifts—which are from thee—and which are mine, not to hide, but to use—mine not to boast of or flaunt, mine not to belittle. But mine to spend—and use and enjoy—to the hilt!

I give thanks for my gifts, Lord—
and in humble acknowledgment, I celebrate my worth!

Amen.

Dear God,

I have another favor to ask.

I have another insight to request.

Enable me to allow my children to recognize *their* gifts, too.

And, Lord, deliver me from "recognizing" them too positively myself—deciding *for them* what their interests are—dictating to them where their strengths are—manipulating.

(Ah, I dislike that *word.* Let me refrain from the deed as well.)

Help my children *know* themselves—assets as well as liabilities. Help them see that they are *gifted* . . . that their gifts are from thee . . . and that their gifts open up all sorts of possibilities for them.

Lord, enable them to celebrate themselves —honestly and freely.

Amen.

It was just a jack-o-lantern on the kitchen table, Lord,—and an old black pot full of apple cider and dry ice—and a three-year-old neighbor child, kneeling on the bathmat and bobbing for an apple.

But it was Holiday! and it was fun. Partly, I suppose, because everybody I saw that night was involved in the same conspiracy of celebration. It gave us a sort of camaraderie—and it was rejuvenating, and fun.

I'm grateful, Lord, for holidays. They come as accents in the even tenor of our living. Some of them, like this one, are just fun. Others have deeper elements—call us to remembrance in other ways.

But they *do* bring us together, Lord! They do bring us to laughter, recall us to levity. We who worry about the past and the future, and who pile up our possessions in bigger barns and who take ourselves so very seriously . . . need such days!

Thank you—
for nonsense—
and childhood—
and holidays—
and the child-within-us-all, come out to play!
Amen.

Dear Lord,

It is a good feeling to be making today's pumpkin pies out of yesterday's jack-o-lantern.

And life is ever thus.

One of the ingredients of all our present moments is the past. It is newly leavened, freshly spiced, and made into something quite different. But its origins are always in That-Which-Was.

I am grateful, Lord, for yesterdays. I am grateful for the experiences of which my past is made. Had I been choosing, I would not have selected all those I've had. Some of them were pretty frightening to me at the time. But today they are part of my pie. They provide the basis from which I can construct my life today.

I am grateful, Lord, that I do not have to wake up, like the goose, in a whole new world every morning. I'm glad there is carry-over to my experience—and the possibility of compounding of each day's learning.

I am grateful.

Amen.

It is not July 25, and the beginning of hurricane season, and I am not in the Virgin Islands. But for me, too, there comes a Supplication Day,

and I, too, come to thee—

"Knee-bowed and body-bent

Before thy throne of grace."

Requesting, beseeching—

making known to thee the prayers of my deepest being.

The winds that batter at my life are not literal hurricane winds, but the battering is as real, and I am as helpless. I come, in supplication.

That for which I pray seems not a great deal to ask—and yet I could not ask *more* of thee.

That for which I pray seems . . . to me . . . to be in accordance with divine will—

and yet, I know that I see through a glass, darkly.

I do not come to thee in anger, or in belligerence, threatening to turn from thee if my supplication is denied. For when I turn from thee, I am bereft.

Thou art God.

But I come earnestly, Lord—requesting, beseeching.

If it be thy will, grant me this. And if not, be with me still.

Amen.

Father,

Little kids really are so neat!

I stand amazed at the things they come up with—they whose effervescence has not yet been overlaid with any varnished veneer of propriety. They who are still honest, still open—still free to scatter their love carelessly, generously, non-exclusively around them.

They are so refreshing . . . and neat!

So enriching! How enlivening a time with them becomes—as though, when I'm with them, *anything* seems possible! Their love is contagious, and I can respond to it. Their laughter is bewitching, and I am bewitched. There is *life* and vigor and enthusiasm in their beings that spills over into mine.

And I am blessed! Thank you, Father—for little kids!

Amen.

Father,
She wrote the thank-you letter—briefly, as befits a seven-year-old. Then she did an illustration on the back. Only it didn't turn out right, and she scribbled through it. Apologetically—she added:

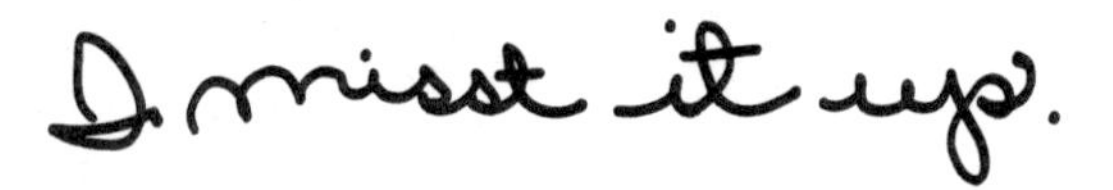

Ah, Father!

Me, too! Some days I really do get things messed up—flubbing opportunities, misreading cues, bungling up the whole works.

And then I get uptight—belittling—castigating—judging myself from *my* perspective.

Funny thing—when she brought me her "misst up" paper, I could look at it from an "older and wiser" point of view. I foresee all sorts of growth and possibility for that little lass! She's becoming!

Father, why do I credit you with less understanding? Surely you look at my blunders from a perspective beyond my comprehension. Surely you accept my errors calmly, and my inept admission with love—encouraging me to move on from here, unburdened by the "misst up papers" of the past.

Amen.

Dear Lord,

I have a cricket on my hearth for company, and a pair of them outside my window for summer song.

I have the smell of strawberries, the sound of windchimes, the feel of a breeze just ruffling my hair. I have a sycamore leaf to look at, coffee perking in cheery blurps, leaf patterns against blue sky, a wisp of cloud to wonder at, a tardy moon still lingering to enjoy the day.

Ah, Lord . . . my cup runneth over!

Every day, *every day,* there are heaping handfuls of things to bring delight into my life. There is some *old* thing, newly seen (like the exquisite little rabbit, with the purple-petaled collar, in every larkspur blossom . . . and to think I was forty before I ever even knew he was there) . . . or some *new* thing, freshly seen—some *teasing* smell, some lovely feel.

And I'm not even counting the big things. These are just the seasonings—but oh, how they flavor my *every* day!

My cup, indeed, runneth over!

Amen.

God,

Where do I get the feeling that an appliance, once purchased, should last forever?

And why . . . why? . . . should I feel personally miffed, and *put upon* . . . if something belonging to *me* should dare to quit functioning? As though I, by "living right," should be exempt from water-heater fatigue or refrigerator breakdown, or even leaks in the hose that goes to the washing machine!

Odd—the way we set ourselves apart as being untouchable by such mundane things. And amusing (but only *afterwards*) when we discover how . . . violate . . . we feel, when mere things do us wrong.

And childish (afterwards), when we get it all back in perspective.

Ah, Lord, "how can we ever be the sold short or the cheated, we who for every service have long ago been overpaid?"

Amen.

Ah, Lord,
How is it that we *talk* more about new diets and uncertain bank accounts and the price of sugar—
than we do about the food crisis facing the whole world—
and we *think* more about cars and football and what's for supper—
than we do about hopelessness in the ghetto and loneliness down the block?

And then we come to you, Lord, wondering at our own inner poverty—surprised that we do not "receive more grace"—troubled that we do not find it easier (after all these years!) to feel thee always near.

Only occasionally, when we turn the TV off long enough, and stem the endless flow of mental *trivia* long enough, does it occur to us that there might be any connection between the focus—and the faith.
Our Father, whose concern and Fatherhood is for *all* persons, stir us from the selfish lethargy which envelops us.
Stir *me,* Lord.

Amen.

Dear Lord,
Is it because she is one of the "television generation" that she expects *all* things to be solvable—*all* crises to come to neat conclusions by the end of the thirty-minute time slot?—and in real life, too?

Is this what makes her so frustrated when things don't turn out neatly, with all the loose ends tucked in—or when things don't turn out at all . . . but just keep drifting on and on and on?

Ah, no wonder. Help me help her understand that life is not so compartmentalized—one problem to solve, or one relationship to iron out by 7:30 so we can switch channels and watch Cannon.

Help us both remember that our problems are not neatly separated episodes, each with its own cast and sponsor—but that they lap over each other, mutually influencing and affecting everything and everybody else. More like soap operas, really, but without the organ music. And without the privilege of turning them off.

But ah, Lord, the *freedom* in not being restricted to thirty-minute all-wrapped-up episodes! Our lives are *not* thus rigidly programmed—*not* thus restricted to predictability. The solutions aren't already written out for us. We are *free* to decide—and free to live out our own stories. Let this freedom not be a frustration for us—for her, for me—but a challenge and a delight. I don't *want* all the loose ends tied up by 7:30. For this isn't "just another dramatic situation." This is my life.

Thank you, Lord.

Amen.

Dear Lord,

She's been a lonely child, I think—and I didn't even know it. Like a middle child, who gets left out sometimes because she's too little to go with "the big kids"—and too big to enjoy playing with the little ones all the time.

Like the child who finds out that she is not "Monday's child, and fair of face"—or even Tuesday's, full of grace . . . but Friday's child. Full of woe. *Destined,* she feels, to be so.

And lonely. And unsure of her place. Unaware that she *has* a special place.

And I didn't even know she felt this way.

I see it now—now that she has finally let that corner of her feelings show. I wonder how she could *not* have known of the special love that I have for her.

I have *told* her.

I have cooked favorite dishes, especially for her, thinking of that as an expression of love.

But I have also heard her talking, and not *listened.*

I have also taken her where she needed to go, and not felt much real *interest* in her project or errand.

I have looked at her as "one of the kids"—and not as her own unique self.

No wonder she wonders.

Ah, Lord, help me *communicate* my awareness of her, of *her,* not just as "my little girl," but as a *person,* in her own right. Help me show respect for her personhood. And help me let her see that my love, which has always *been,* for her, continues now, and grows, for the person she is becoming.

Special place? Indeed!

How grateful I am for *this* one, Lord!

Amen.

Lord,

Was Marx right? *Is* our faith an opiate? I think you never *meant* it so—never intended that we should use faith in you as an escape . . . or a pain-killer, as a way of lifting ourselves right up out of the problems of the real world, that we might rest on cloudy beds of ease . . . untroubled and untouched.

Forgive us when we so abuse our relationship with thee.

Forgive *me,* when I come to thee seeking numbness. Make me *more* sensitive, Lord—not less so, more awake—not less so. Let me hurt not only with my own pain but also with the hurts of others who, because they belong to thee, belong also to me.

Forgive that feebleness of spirit that makes me ever want to forget, or escape. And give me clarity of mind, sensitivity of spirit, and a wide-awakeness that embraces all the reality I can hold . . . in thy name, which is to say because I love.

Amen.

Dear Lord,

She is a person of disconcerting honesty, and sometimes her comments leave me exposed . . .
especially to myself.

That's uncomfortable—which, I suppose, is why I avoided her. I never did like having my lovely pipe dreams and my little self-delusions pricked.

But, Lord, how grateful I have become, for her. For she is a person of arresting clarity. And when my needs are real, it is with her that I like to talk.

I give thanks that among my friends there is one who tells it, not like she thinks I'd like to hear it, but like she sees it. Her disconcerting honesty is strength and support to me, and Lord, I am grateful indeed for her love.

I had not realized the psychological impact of a FOR SALE sign in the front yard—until some goofy kid hammered one firmly into ours, last night—and I looked out, as I made the final bedtime check on things—and saw it.

Ah, Lord, I've *talked* about being free . . . free to go wherever I might be useful . . . free to move, if need be, to a whole new place.

But I never meant it. I didn't know, until I saw the sign, that I hadn't meant it. I didn't know, until I saw the sign, how grateful I've been, these almost eleven years, for the opportunity of staying in one place—for the peaceful opportunity of putting down my roots. I didn't know how unwilling I have become to disturb their growth. Let me not get so entwined in house-roots that I become rigid and unmovable.

Strange, how the roots that I *value* most are not always the ones I *tend* best. The tangible ones so obviously *have* to be tended that . . .

Oh, Lord, forgive! Except for you, *nothing* else is valid!

Ah, let me realize that the roots I value most are not in this house, nor in a plot of ground—but in the Ground of My Being.

And it is only the roots that are in thee that nourish my soul.

Amen.

The times are hard, Lord—beans and cheese are up again—sugar now unconsiderable—and no end in sight. What's to become of us?

It has never really occurred to me before that I might go hungry. *Be* hungry? Yes—briefly, when it's nearing supper time, and I'm half past ready. But *go* hungry? No. Not us. Not me. I never *have*—and never expected to.

Until recently. Now it occurs to me.

And what about the others, whose too-small pensions don't have any cost-of-living clause? Whose jobs, which seemed so *sure* after all these years, have suddenly ceased to exist? They begin not just to *contemplate* hunger but to *experience* it.

And I, who still have cans of soup and tuna on my shelf, and jars of flour and sugar in my cabinet, do precious little to be of help to anyone else. I am not thinking of the invisible hosts of the hunger-haunted in Ethiopia and Bangladesh, but of my *visible* neighbors, whose need is near.

The times are hard, Lord. Be thou our strength. And so touch our hearts that we may be strength and sustenance to each other. Let *me* seek out practical ways to share my more-than-enough with those whose all is not sufficient. Let me not react to the specter of hunger by hoarding, but by sharing, as I have never, really, shared before.

Amen.

Forgive, Lord. I haven't the right to *not* think of the "invisible" hosts of the hunger-haunted in Ethiopia and Bangladesh—or wherever else in the world masses starve.

They are not invisible, for I see their faces in my morning paper. They are not distant, for our world has grown small. And I cannot—*must* not—shut them out of my thinking.

We make long-range plans for easing the world's hunger crisis. ("But my child is starving *now.*") We hold a world food conference and invite the participation of the nations. (And how many persons die, while a conference is going on?) And *I* sit with my tray in front of the TV, and watch the starving, weary, misshapen children, and never miss a bite.

Lord, forgive. Forgive my waste, and forgive my blind oblivion.

There must *be* long-range plans—or millions *more* will starve in the future. But I am too willing to let the fact that *I'm* not at the conference free me from any responsibility at all. Forgive. And haunt me . . . with faces and facts . . . until I write my congressmen and send my tithe. (*Tithe,* Lord? A *tenth,* when people starve and die?)

Forgive. And burden me with painful sensitivity —with personal responsibility—for what's going on in my world.

Amen.

Now—while I feel the burden—
let me do something about it—
take some action—undertake some
specific. For if I do not, *now,* the
hurt and the burden will begin to go away

—and I will have found some way of justifying (or overlooking) my non-participation.

And *another* child will have
died.

Ah, Lord,

I give grateful recognition and special thanks this day for the fact that frugality can be fun! (Which is not—you know!—why I began to practice it.)

But the economic pressures which have made belt-tightening mandatory have brought certain new pleasures into my day.

There is a special delight in having made my youngest a patchwork skirt—out of scraps, and an old zipper: total cost, nil.

There is a special pride in being able to convert "*that* old dress" into *neat* summer pajamas for one of the kids—in having brought off a really *good* supper for 17¢ per serving—in having *made* the Christmas gifts, out of wood scraps from the garage and cloth scraps from the rag bag, out of flour and paper and leftover paint.

I thank you, Lord, for the fun that can be found in "making do" with what we have—for the puzzle, the challenge, the *bonus* accrued from being thrown back on our own resources, and finding them adequate!

Life is good, in prosperity and in adversity. It's goodness is not measured in how "nice" things are, or in how easy—but its goodness is *there,* for me to find, whatever the circumstances. I have been offered abundant life. God, forbid that I should ever think of that in economic terms.

Amen.

Part of our problem, Lord, is that none of us was ever really trained for trouble.

We learned something about how to remove stains, and to make a meatloaf, but nothing at all about how to cope with a brain tumor—or a wandering spouse—or a self-destructing child.

We weren't really trained for trouble, and it catches us vulnerable.

Hmmm. That's not altogether true.

Every muscle that we have flexed has been strengthened in the flexing, against the time when we should need it.

And every moment that we have spent with thee, is preparation for whatever lies ahead—even if some of that "whatever" be heavy trouble.

When the times come that try our souls, we find ourselves coping, wondering even as we do, how we could.

"How we could" is because of your strengthening presence, Lord. You have not promised that all would be easy, but you have assured us of your presence—whatever the trial.

Trained for trouble? Well, no. But accompanied, trouble or no, by the Creator of all that is!

Ah, Lord, we cope, because we do not have to do so alone.

For me, there is no other way.

Thank you, Lord, my God.

Amen.

Yea, though I walk through meadows of sunlight or valleys of shadow, thou art with me!

Father, God,

There are times when I would like to be able to tell you how much you mean to me—when I yearn to *say* my love—to show my love—when my heart is full, and my cup runneth over—either of joy, or anxiety, or grief or pain—

and I *yearn* to come to you as I came to my father when I was a child—when I needed the comfort of his arm around my shoulder—needed his strength—needed the assurance of *his* expressed love to understand the depth of my own.

These are the times when I want you to be a physical, touchable being—not a spirit. Because what I understand best is the tangible.

And yet—

I cannot really, ultimately, want to reduce you to my comprehension. It's just that there are times when I yearn to tell you that I love you, and yearn to know that you know—and I'm not sure how.

Ah, Lord. I delude myself again. There are ways of *showing* you my love—as surely as there are ways of showing the members of my family that they are dear to me. And I deceive myself if I think I'm *not* showing you, every day,

by the way I live out that day,

whether or not . . .

and how much . . . I love you.

And though I wish for times when we could talk, as humans talk, I am aware of a deeper level of communication.

Ah, Lord, it is true that I don't know how to love thee . . . but insofar as I *do* know, accept my love, and enable the increase.

Amen.

Father, forgive us our conformity.
We abuse the word if we translate being
"made in thy image" to mean
being "molded into the same pattern,"
For "thy image" is not a pre-set shape,
into which we are cast.
Thy image is a freedom,
an open-to-lifeness
a sensitivity
an attitude of love-without-strings
and these are not attributes that can be confined within a mold.

Forgive the time I spend trying to shove my days into preconceived shapes—trying to conform—blindly doing that which fits me poorly, simply because someone else considers it proper—and let me be me.
Let me enjoy—and celebrate!—the freedom to be the me that I was created to be.

Amen!

Dear Lord,

I'd like to see this child of mine learn how to *tackle* a problem . . .

it's so much easier not to—

so much easier, at the moment, not to face a difficult situation.

And so much harder, in the long run, to keep on living with the haunting presence of the untackled problem.

I'd like to see him learn to acknowledge his difficult situations—face them, squarely—think them through—

and then deal with them.

The ability to do this is part of our *human*ness, Lord—part of your gift to us, that we *can* grapple with circumstances—that we *can* see . . . and decide . . . and take wise action (or take no action, if that's where wise decision points us). Other creatures can only drift. But we can choose.

Help him choose, Lord. Help him learn that he has the right to exercise his options.

And help him learn that to make his decisions in the presence of the Lord of all things, can give him a clarity, and a strength, to see them through.

Amen.

P.S.

Me, too, Lord.

Dear Lord—
Ground of our hope—
we do affirm our faith in thee—
we do affirm our faith in the goodness of thy creation.
And we do affirm our faith in the possibilities within our own lives.

We are aware of the problems that trouble our world—of stark hunger—of continuing discreet preparation for war (and of a mind-set that sees war as "solution")—of depression not only of economy, but of mind and of spirit.

We are aware of the problems that trouble our own souls—of the paucity of our faith, and of the withholding of our response to thee.

But the world has been troubled—deeply troubled—before. And out of its darkest moments have come new revelations of thy nature, and of thy plan.

We do affirm a plan. Faith affirms it, and integrity demands that we prepare ourselves for whatever it may require of us.

It is not ours to know the secrets of the future. It *is* ours to prepare ourselves to live in that future. And so,

in affirmation of faith, and of hope, and of possibilities, we covenant with thee.

Amen, and amen.